Ooh, visitors!..

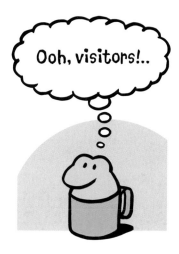

To Jill, because love and laughter nurture each other.

Welcome to Yellowberry Hill

published by
Barzipan Publishing

an imprint of Medina Publishing Ltd
310 Ewell Road
Surbiton
Surrey KT6 7AL

ISBN: 978-1-9997633-3-6

© Mark Mowforth 2017

Printed and bound by Interak Printing House, Poland

Mark Mowforth asserts his moral right to be identified as the author of this book.
CIP Data: A catalogue record for this book is available at the British Library.
All rights reserved. No part of this book may be reproduced, stored in a retrieval system, or transmitted in any form or by any means, electronic, mechanical, photocopying, recording, or otherwise, without the prior permission of the copyright owners.

Welcome to a place where an owl in a onesie, a snake in a cape and a mole with a conspicuous wig are best friends: A place where a cat has a pet dog, a frog is permanently in a mug and the local moose is never without a slice of pie. This is Yellowberry Hill! Here you'll also find an undersized panda regularly testing the patience of a duck in a woolly hat, while a little blue fish tries to make sense of it all and a distant yak looks on. Once you've accepted that all this is normal, you'll be right at home...

I think there must be some sort of panic on at work...
...I had a text from my boss this morning about getting myself over there...
I ignored it - there's no way I'm going in on a Sunday!
It's Monday.
Marks

Oh dear...are you okay?..
Yeah, could be worse...
...my arm's mainly just bruised and the chocolate milkshake should wash out of my fur.
Do you want to buy a stupid hammock?

Did you once say that true friends say 'we' not 'I' when they talk with each other?
Wow! I'm really touched that you remember!...I did say exactly that!
Okay, cool.
I've borrowed your we-pad.

Everything alright?
Sort of...
...I need to set a password for this website...
...I'm trying to think of a book which only features a few people...
....I put in 'WarandPeace' and it said 'too many characters'.

That's a nice story about the squirrel brothers.
Yeah.
Reminds you of what's really important.
Now I think about it, my family are always there for me, and I'm always here for them.
Same here.
That way we never actually have to meet up.

Warm Hat Duck

Tidy, loyal and a bit of an over-thinker, Warm Hat Duck is often the one trying to take things seriously; the all-too-regular look of mild despair on his earnest little face is a sign of how well this is going.

The warm hat in question is intended to keep the wearer's brain at optimum thinking temperature, but this doesn't stop its owner from having many hapless and absent-minded moments, and it hasn't helped at all with the endless task of trying to figure out Quite Small Panda.

Likes…cheese straws, anything that goes 'click' in a satisfying way when you press it, crosswords.

Doesn't like…roller-coasters, wobbly tables, having too many choices.

Took a long detour round the lake as the foot-bridge is closed for repairs. Sometimes I forget I'm a duck.

Had my first driving lesson today.
Excellent! Talk me through it!..
Well, we pulled out of the car park...
...and I stopped to let a snail cross the road...
Then what?
That's all we had time for.

I'll get the coffees - do you need me to explain what the different types are?
I'm not that ill-informed you know!..
...I'll have a 'cup of chino'.
Just been to a conference on bouncy castle storage. Bit of a let-down.

It's hard being single sometimes.
All my owl friends seem to be in couples ...lots of lovey-dovey looks...lots of kissing - don't think they realise how annoy-ingly cliquey it is.
Yeah, that's the beaks I suppose.
Eh?!
Bound to make kissing annoy-ingly clicky.
Markm

Stupid laptop! ...the 'r' and 'd' are stuck!

...worst possible time! There's a mistake now in the job application I sent to 'Elite Bakeries'...

...it's supposed to end with 'my ambition is a job that lets me go home full of pride'.

Last word reads 'pie'.

Quite Small Panda

One of a kind, Quite Small Panda is well known at Yellowberry Hill for his very frequent diet and attitude malfunctions and love of sleep....although if you were to ask him, he'd say 'I only have the average 7 or 8 hours. Same again at night.'

Quite Small Panda's main goals at the moment are to find a new job and to learn to drive; both of these are proving more than a little challenging, and progress so far has been a case of 'two steps forward and one step back', but without the first bit.

Likes...breakfast, elevenses, lunch, snacks, dinner, supper, comfy beds, fireworks.

Doesn't like...waking up, getting up, ukuleles.

Those automated checkouts are getting too smart. Bought some celery yesterday and it said 'unexpected item in bagging area'.

Got to have a meeting with my boss tomorrow about my 'attitude'.
Oh dear - what prompted that?
The lunch on our team building day - I finished all the soup before some people could have any.
My boss said 'what've we been saying?... there's no 'I' in 'team'!'
What did you say?
'No, but there's a 'mine' in 'minestrone''

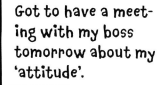

Mmm - those cakes look lovely.
What's the book?
Self help.
I see...
...based on the idea that if you'd rather not get help from a counsellor, then you...
...help yourself.
Why, thank you.

How's your listening skills course at work going?
Part 1 was pretty good...
...Part 2 was on Tuesday but I missed it.
I thought they said Thursday.

Hi Mum and Dad,
I hope all is well.

You know we were
talking about
things that look
tricky to control
using just a tail?

You were
right about
that drone.

I've got an interview for a job that's come up in accounts...will you help me prepare?
Sure...how?
Just fire a typical inter-view question at me.
Okay...
How would you describe yourself in 3 words?
'Highly numerate'.

Snake in a Cape

Undeterred by some rather alarming incidents involving brambles, high winds and revolving doors, our stylish friend simply can't imagine life without a cape - the ever-satisfying swoop factor alone makes it worth all the jeopardy.

Snake in a Cape's other trademark is the talent he's, er, 'blessed' with for using day-to-day events as opportunities for creating snappy jokes....thankfully, these are often channelled into his stand-up routines at his favourite venue, the Octopus Club ('They know how to clap!').

Likes...seeing the funny side of things, toast, spontaneous get-togethers.

Doesn't like...camping, DIY, sitting backwards on trains.

Watched a squirrel selling mirrors this morning. I thought 'I could see myself doing that'.

Been into town?
Yeah, I had to take my iron back to the shop as a really weird thing happened...
...it had grown to twice it's size!
Wow.... what did they say?
It's scaled up.

Hmm... 'Tuesday Jones'...
...would you name a child after the day they were born on?
Nah...
...it was a real blight for Uncle Bin Day.

Did I see you going to a yoga class with a leopard yesterday?
Ah yes, bit of an error...
...I was supposed to take my own leotard.

Apparently it's very easy to confuse seconds with minutes on my new micro-wave. Quick hello and thanks to all the fire fighters I met today.

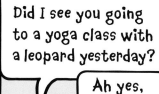

How did the job interview go?
Not very well...
...I'm beginning to think that there are just no good answers to some of the ques-tions they ask.
Like what?
Like 'Is this the first interview you've fallen asleep in?'
Marko

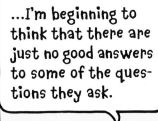

Interesting look...
I'm off to a pirate fancy-dress party...
...this is what they used to wear on their heads.
One of us needs to talk to Very Puzzled Fish about his 'bandana'.

Onesie Owl

Very Puzzled Fish recently asked Onesie Owl a question he'd been pondering for a while; 'Do you have any problems trying to fly in a Onesie?' 'Not really', came the reply, 'Though some airlines get a bit sniffy when I go business class'.

Onesie Owl's particular combination of comfy day wear and canny attitude to life mean he's always contentedly warm and effortlessly cool. So cool, in fact, that Snake in a Cape has now made it his mission to come up with a joke that'll actually get him 'in hoots'....

Likes...understanding things, afternoon naps, old films.

Doesn't like...glove puppets, mustard, trampolining.

Some people don't think things through - whose idea was it to release all those balloons at the end of the 'Hedgehog of the Year' awards?...

Got to go to Yellowberry Vale tomorrow - thought I'd take the train.
You'll be in familiar company - Warm Hat Duck says that train's owly.
...or 'hourly'?..

My driving lesson didn't go too well today - got stuck on this stupid round-about for ages.
You'd think people would be kinder to a learner though.
Did someone get annoyed?
Yeah.
The owner of the fairground.

Went to see my cousin yesterday - loves his job but works all hours. Not much time for going out and having fun if you're a chocalatier.
You haven't listened to a word I've been saying, have you?
Yes...
...your cousin can't go out in the sun because he has a chocolate ear.

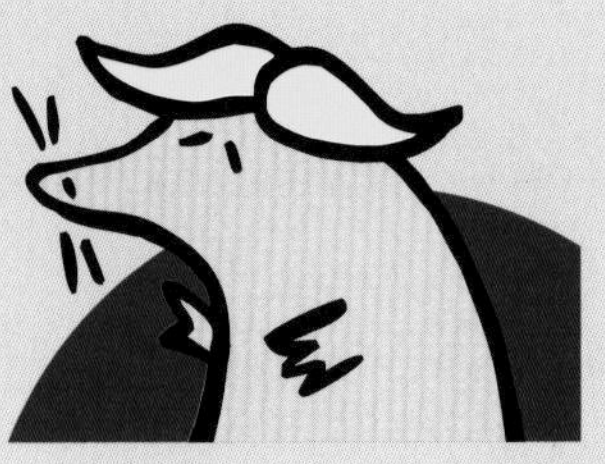

Wigmole

An enthusiastic amateur artist with a love of language and the big ideas of life, Wigmole is wiser and more thoughtful than his questionable choice of hairpiece might suggest.

Wigmole has been told that his 'look' appears to have been copied by the odd person keen to get on in the world, which, luckily, he takes as a form of compliment. In any case, little bothers him once he's out on the hills with his easel – aside from uninvited comments on his work by annoying pandas.

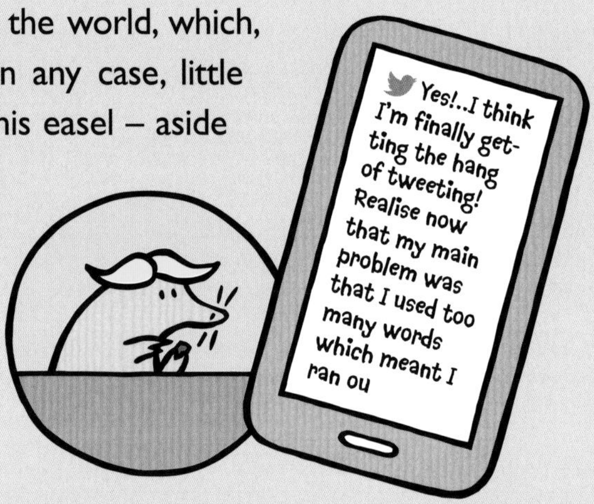
Yes!..I think I'm finally getting the hang of tweeting! Realise now that my main problem was that I used too many words which meant I ran ou

Likes... a nice view, well-made socks, uniqueness.

Doesn't like... unproductive days, perforated things that don't tear properly, hiccups.

Hi Wigmole - haven't seen you for a while..
No - I've been on an acting course.
Oh? While you were away I went on a diet!
I noticed! You look really great!
Thanks.
Good course then?
Can you tell?...

Look! I got a box of cakes on special offer!
Near their use-by date, but all okay.
Best before?...
...anyone else gets here!

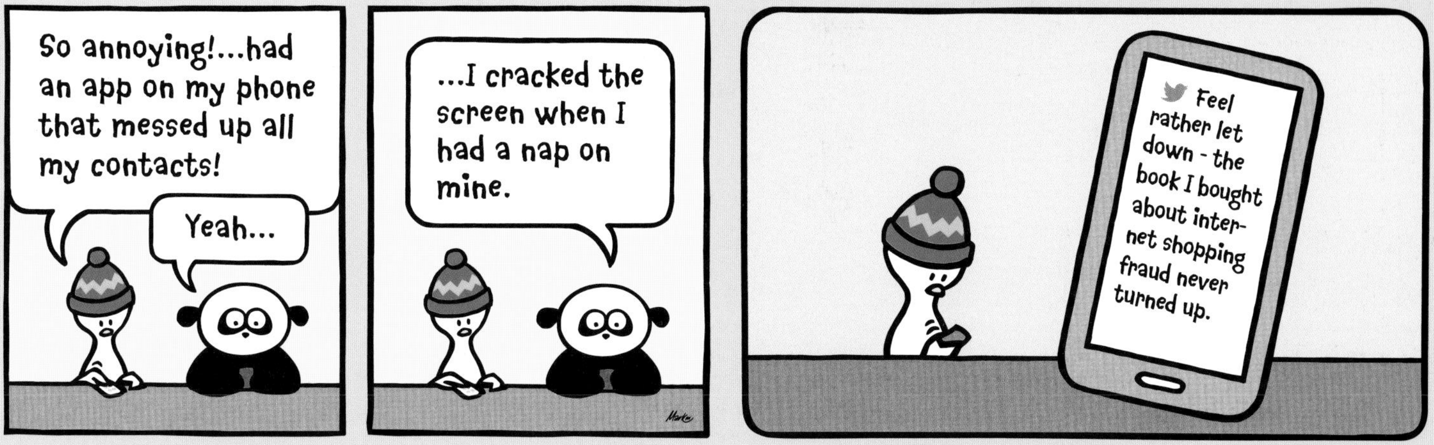
So annoying!...had an app on my phone that messed up all my contacts!
Yeah...
...I cracked the screen when I had a nap on mine.
Feel rather let down - the book I bought about inter-net shopping fraud never turned up.

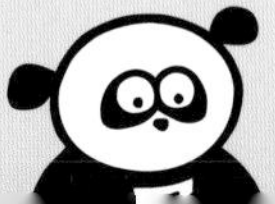

This dispute of yours isn't really worth it for a few pounds... I'd write one more letter and then draw a line under it.
The wording's okay.. ..but why the jungle scene?
You said draw a lion under it.

Just heard about that job....I didn't get it.

Sorry to hear that...

... but do you remember that advice I gave you?..'When one door closes another one opens'.

That was advice?..

...I thought you were talking about that rubbish car you bought.

Fell asleep on the train from Yellow-berry Vale yester-day....woke up at Sandy Halt!
Easily done - I fell asleep on the journey to work this morning.
Oh?...
...when did you wake up?
When I fell off my bike.

Moose n' Pie

Living, quite contentedly, in a slightly alternative pie-centred world, Moose n' Pie is steady, unflappable and laid-back.

The preferred mode of transport for our serene friend is a bicycle, though this is not without its issues, as his twitter followers learnt when he told them that 'a very kind doctor in A&E patched me up and gave me some excellent advice; if you're eating a pie and riding a bike, don't wave'. This is now his second favourite saying, after 'reach for the stars… but don't drop your pie'.

Likes…well, that's obvious. Also comic books and bonsai trees.

Doesn't like…planning ahead, rushing, plastic cutlery.

Just been to cheer up my bull friend after his fifth job rejection. Who'd have thought it was so hard to get a job in a china shop?

What on earth is that?!
Lunch.
...a waffle, a doughnut and some fries?!
...you don't know anything about balancing the diff-erent food groups, do you!?
Well look again Mr. Cocky...
...I think you'll see I have a square thing, a round thing and some long thin things.

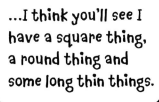

Interesting programme on tonight about synesthesia.
What's that?
It's when you see things like numbers as colours - often associated with high intelligence and creativity.
Hmmm.
On too late for me.
I'm usually in bed by yellow o'clock.

Wow! Have you been to the gym?!
Yup - thought I'd finally give it a go...
....had a few sessions in the big glass rotater thing, now I'm off to chill out!
Who'd have thought!
Yeah...
...maybe next time he'll get further than the revolving doors.

Well, I learnt a couple of things today...

...for one, the airbag in my driving instructors car goes off in your face after only a minor bump...

Oh dear...

...and?...

...nobody notices when I have two black eyes.

Very Puzzled Fish

Here, you might think, is someone ideally suited to 'going with the flow', but sadly this isn't the case…

Even the simplest aspects of life can prove endlessly baffling to Very Puzzled Fish, like the postcard from his aunt saying her holiday hotel was 'nothing to write home about'.

Thankfully, Very Puzzled Fish's Yellowberry Hill friends are all kind and understanding types - though one cheeky individual did convince him he needed to stop posting photos to facebook because 'the internet's full'.

Likes…things that make sense, liquorice torpedoes, summer.

Doesn't like…revolving doors, sharks, sudden change.

That memory foam pillow I tried is useless - I still forgot my sister's birthday.

Very Puzzled Fish seems a bit low - he was off to find some-one to cheer him up this morning.
Hi.
Hi.
So...I found out the difference between an op-timist and an optometrist.

Sometimes I think there are too many atttention-seekers in the world.
Me too.
Hmm - the builder working on my new porch is one of them.
Really?
Yeah...
...likes to make an entrance!

Went on a course today about 'stock management and demand prediction' but I don't think the trainers knew their stuff.
Why?
There weren't enough biscuits.
Think my piano teacher fancies me - said my scales were lovely!

Any plans for the summer?
A few...
...my niece is going to be with me for a while, so we've got various things on the cards.
Hee hee!...
...I bet you're making the most of the peace before that little terror turns up!
Harsh.

Frog in a Mug

Everyone at Yellowberry Hill enjoys an occasional catch-up over a nice mug of frog - especially as the frog in question is easy-going and good company.

Snake in a Cape is always especially pleased if Frog in a Mug is around as he knows that at least one person will be enjoying his particular brand of humour. Also, with 4687 brothers and sisters, there are a fair number of nephews and nieces for Frog in a Mug to stay in touch with (...or, as a certain caped character put it, 'keep a handle on'...)

Likes... being with friends, sudoku, a good joke.

Doesn't like... pistachio nuts, yodeling, food made into a face.

Went to get a book on frogspawn to help my nephew with a project. Librarian threw me out - thought I said frog's porn.

I wish I was more confident. I went on an assertiveness course last week but it didn't help at all - it was rubbish.
Did you tell them?
...in no uncertain terms!
??
?
Oh hang on, I see what you're thinking...

Took my laptop to the repair shop today.

I was sat in the park using it and I noticed that the screen had gone dim.

They explained the problem very considerately.

What was it?

My sunglasses.

I've been sent some photos of me at that wedding I went to.
I'm rubbish at having my picture taken...
...I spoilt this one because I looked round.
I'd say you look pretty round in all of them.

If you were backing up a car and your driving instructor kept saying 'two metres...two metres!' what would you think it meant?
...that's how much space you had?..
Exactly!
Wow!...have you seen those two bent parking meters?!..

Cat with a Dog

Creative, sharp and insightful, Cat with a Dog's calm and well-grounded nature forms an interesting contrast to that of her mildly bonkers dog. Her patience and understanding recently came in especially handy when explaining to Very Puzzled Fish about the refurbishment of the shop she runs – he couldn't quite grasp how a vintage and retro shop could be updated.

Cat with a Dog enjoys daily walks around Yellowberry Hill, and these often prove unexpectedly entertaining...

Likes...trying new things, a good day out, skating.

Doesn't like...that bit in a TV programme about what's coming up, thoughtlessness, itchy wool.

Didn't realise how enthusiastic my dog had become about fetching sticks till today's fiasco at the archery contest.

You're out early!
Yup - been to Wigmole's to borrow this...
...it's for this great new job I'm applying for...
...'Confident phone manner'...check!... 'General experience of IT packages'...check!..
...just need to work on my keyboard skills.

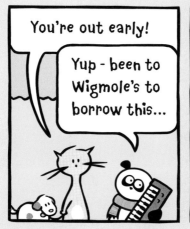

Look...this is my grandad and his brother with their father, uncle and grandfather.
Wow, that's a great photo to have!...
'The gathering of the forebears'.
Five.

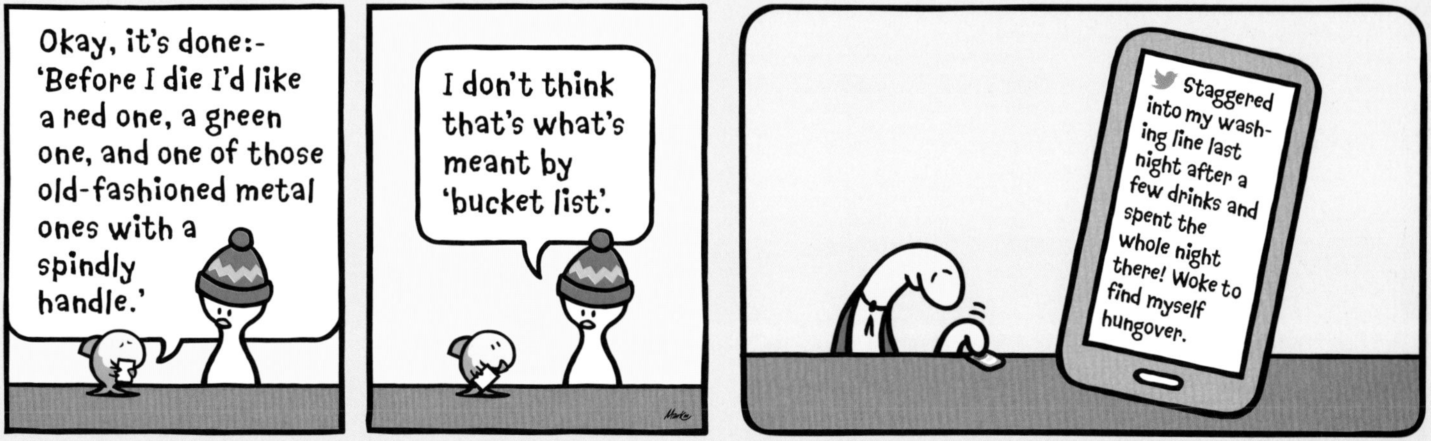
Okay, it's done:- 'Before I die I'd like a red one, a green one, and one of those old-fashioned metal ones with a spindly handle.'
I don't think that's what's meant by 'bucket list'.
Staggered into my washing line last night after a few drinks and spent the whole night there! Woke to find myself hungover.

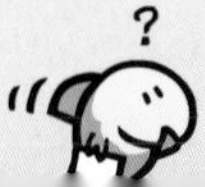

How was the talk last night on Pirates?
Not what I was expecting.
It was mostly about all these exercises they used to do. We joined in a lot though.
I think you've been to a pilates class.

Can we stop now? I'm hungry.
At least finish the question - you have to know this stuff if you really want this pro-motion..
...is the answer 'annual turnover', 'profit and loss' or 'supply of cash'.
Sorry, all I heard was 'apple turnover,' 'profiteroles' and 'pie & mash'.

Background Yak

There's nothing Background Yak likes more than spending time out and about so he can see what's unfolding in the big old world. As a result of his many hours outdoors, he's been rewarded with some rare and amazing sights: He once saw Quite Small Panda leaving for work on time.

Our perma-scarfed friend will happily tell you that, if you want a wise perspective on the madness of life, the background is an excellent place to find it. Of course, if we all take his advice and join him, it won't actually be the background any more. Tricky.

Likes...early morning, the sea, humming.

Doesn't like...karaoke, velcro, unfriendliness.

Had to send my DIY book back - apparently it doesn't mean Daily Inspiration for Yaks.

Morning, Onesie Owl.
Morning, Cat with a Dog.
Cheesy puffs are on special offer again today.
How do you know?
You'll see.

I need a new pillow but there are so many different types ...hollow fibre...down ...microbead...foam...
...rice.
Rice?!
I guess - why else would there be pillow rice?
Pilau rice!..
Can't be very comfy.
Mark

I think I need to pay more attention to emails at work.
Hmmm.
Did I hear that your company's moved offices?
Yeah. That's what I mean.
I don't know where they've gone.

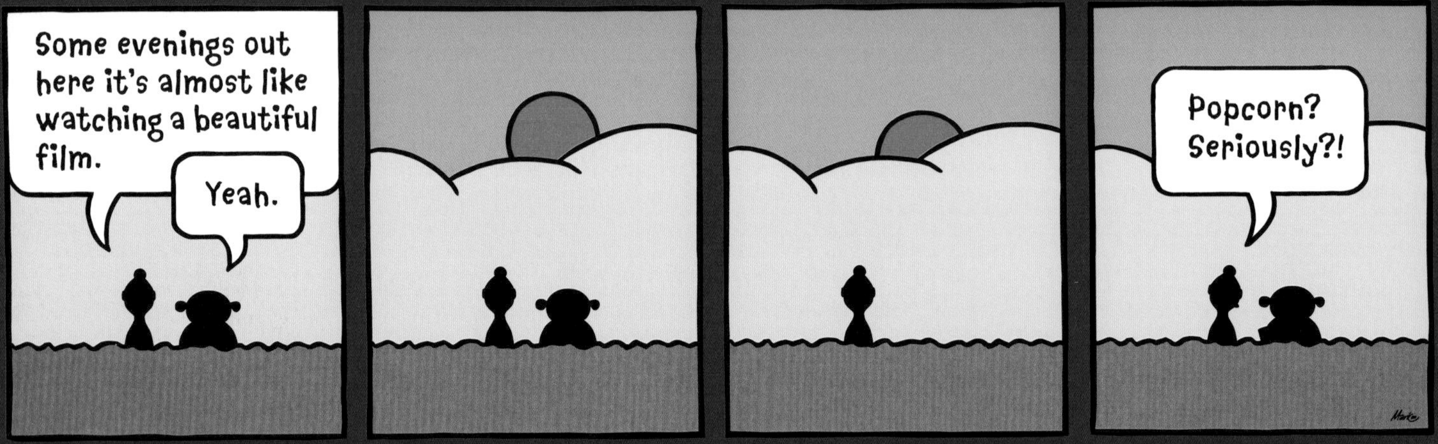
Some evenings out here it's almost like watching a beautiful film.
Yeah.
Popcorn? Seriously?!

So... will a certain panda ever pass his driving test...or get a new job...or even track down his existing one? Will Snake in a Cape finally hit on a joke that even Onesie Owl can't help laughing at? How many more pirate parties will that little blue fish go to with a banana on his head?...

If you'd like to keep following the Yellowberry Hill story, you can visit us at our online home, yellowberryhill.com and sign up for free regular email strips... or stay in touch with the gentle madness through social media. Thanks for dropping by!

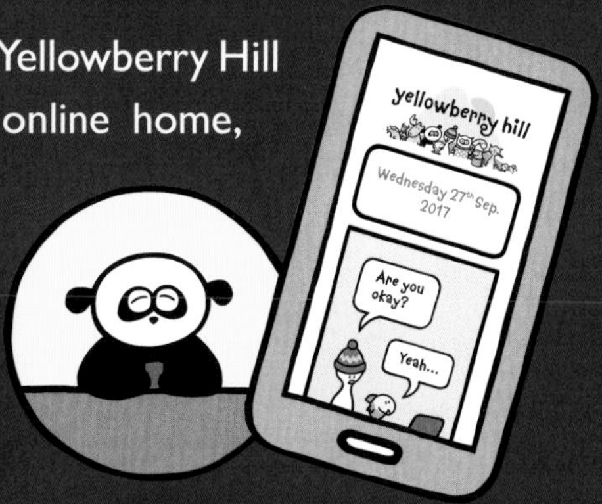
yellowberry hill
Wednesday 27th Sep. 2017
Are you okay?
Yeah...